Carving the Native American Face

Terry Kramer

Text written with
and photography by
Douglas Congdon-Martin

Schiffer Publishing Ltd®

4880 Lower Valley Road Atglen, Pennsylvania 19310

DEDICATION

I dedicate this book to my wife Kay, whose help and 100% support has made it possible for me to pursue my artistic career. Kay does with expertise all of the non-artist type activities that need to be accomplished so that I can pursue my art. Kay works with the patrons, keeps contact with the galleries and gift shops, juries for and schedules shows and demonstrations, arranges classes and seminars, and does hundreds of other activities that keep me going. In short: I am the artist; she runs the business; together we make quite a team. Thank you Kay!

I also thank our friend Shirley Hampton of Salem, Oregon for helping us get started on our artistic journey. In 1977, Shirley and Kay convinced me to enter the Salem Art Fair. That event was the first public showing of my work. Shirley, I appreciate your belief in my ability as an artist and your realization of the existence of my potential as an exhibitor and demonstrating artist. Thank you for taking the time and energy to help us on our journey.

Copyright © 1995 by Terry Kramer

ISBN: 978-0-88740-715-4
Printed in China

Kramer, Terry.
    Carving the native American face / Terry Kramer: text written with and photography by Douglas Congdon-Martin.
        p. cm.
    ISBN: 978-0-88740-715-4
    1. Wood-carving-Technique. 2. Face in art. 3. Indians of North America-
-Pictorial works. I. Congdon-Martin, Douglas. II. Title.
TT199.7.K72   1995
731'.82--dc20   95-1299
                        CIP

Schiffer Books are available at special discounts for bulk purchases for sales promotions or premiums. Special editions, including personalized covers, corporate imprints, and excerpts can be created in large quantities for special needs. For more information contact the publisher:

Published by Schiffer Publishing Ltd.
4880 Lower Valley Road
Atglen, PA 19310
Phone: (610) 593-1777; Fax: (610) 593-2002
E-mail: Info@schifferbooks.com

CONTENTS

INTRODUCTION 3
TOOLS AND LIGHT 6
CARVING THE FACE 8
THE GALLERY 48

For the largest selection of fine reference books on this and related subjects, please visit our web site at: www.schifferbooks.com
We are always looking for people to write books on new and related subjects. If you have an idea for a book please contact us at the above address.
This book may be purchased from the publisher. Include $5.00 for shipping. Please try your bookstore first.
You may write for a free catalog.

In Europe, Schiffer books are distributed by
Bushwood Books
6 Marksbury Ave.
Kew Gardens
Surrey TW9 4JF England
Phone: 44 (0) 20 8392 8585; Fax: 44 (0) 20 8392 9876
E-mail: info@bushwoodbooks.co.uk
Website: www.bushwoodbooks.co.uk

INTRODUCTION

The human face is one of the most looked at and most studied subjects in the life of every seeing person. As children cradled in our mother's arms, or juveniles studying our face in the mirror looking for new pimples, or adults shaving or putting on makeup, we have been subconsciously studying the human face. During every interaction with another individual, we study the face. The face gives us the best source of information about what another person is thinking or feeling. The face is the most powerful conveyor of emotion in the world. Yet, carving the human face is one of the most difficult tasks a carver undertakes. Everyone is familiar with the human face, therefore the carved face is one of the easiest subjects for ourselves and others to use to evaluate the skill the carver. It is the one subject that if executed well, will be greatly appreciated, but if executed poorly, will immediately reveal the carver's lack of skill. A carver cannot fake faces.

Every human face contains basic similarities. The size and shape of the head, the facial planes, and the individual details of the facial features may differ slightly, but there is a basic structure which all faces have in common. Once you master the basic structure, you will be able to carve any face.

This book is about carving a realistic face and has been specifically designed to address the topic of basic facial structure. For it's subject it uses the Native American Indian face as a model.

The face to be carved will be carved in full relief. When carving a realistic face, it is easiest to achieve the look of realism if you carve your face in full relief. Because most carvers make their faces too flat, it is best to do full relief faces before attempting any other type. When a face is too flat, it looks distorted, especially when viewed from any angle other than straight on. Once the face appears distorted, it no longer looks realistic.

How I Came to Carve Indian Faces.

As far back as I can remember, there has existed within me a fascination with the early days of the American West. As a child, every book in the school library written about Indians, trappers, scouts, wagon trains, etc. drew me like a magnet. My imagination took me on war parties, buffalo hunts, fur trapper's rendezvous, wagon trains, and on and on. From the top of my bed, with a pillow for cover and a cap gun for protection, I fought off the onslaught of the white man.

I have always had an innate love of the broad prairies, the American eagle, the big wooly buffalo, tepees, bows and arrows, tomahawks, moccasins, tanned skins, ceremonial items, any thing connected to the culture of the North American Indian. I cannot explain this obsession, but it persists to this very day. This, in the most part, led me to the carving of Indian faces. I do know that I am not alone with these interests. Through my art I have met hundreds of others who have a similar fascination and a similar background in their lives. For proof of this fascination, simply look in any periodical that contains pictures of the carving of numerous artists or go to a carving show and you will find a high percentage of carvings of Indian busts and carvings related to The North American Indian culture.

While I cannot say why I started carving Indian faces, I do know the exact circumstances that got me started. I had been carving stylized faces in driftwood for about a year when one day I visited a high quality Indian art gallery located in downtown Portland. Along with the bronzes and oil paintings there were wood carvings of Indian faces that had been carved in what looked like old fence posts. I was absolutely mesmerized by the carvings which were much more expensive than my budget would allow, but I resolved that I would have one of these carvings. From that day on whenever I got to Portland I would visit the gallery, or, more precisely, the carvings. I found out that they were carved by an artist from Montana and from the bark of large old growth cotton wood trees, not fence posts.

Several months passed, when I found myself and five fellow workers in the Portland airport bound for Atlanta to attend a conference. In the airport lobby there was a glass case and in this case was a display from the western art gallery featuring a cotton wood Indian face carving. Over the months I had begun to think that perhaps I could carve my own face as I was already a carver. Circumstance now found me standing in front of this case with pad and pencil in hand sketching the carving for future reference. As I was drawing, a man wearing a very expensive looking business suit, carrying an impressive looking brief case, walked up beside me. He looked at what I was doing and said,"So you think you can carve that?" Without hesitation I replied, "No, I don't think I can carve that!" It must have been the way I replied because he then said, "Oh! You *know* you can carve that." "That's right," I replied. On that note, he walked away and I walked over to my traveling companions and brought them to the case. As they looked at Indian face staring out at them, I announced that in one year from that day I would be carving better faces than the one in the case. They all laughed. One year later, I took an Indian face that I had carved to work and they did not laugh but shook their head in agreement with what had been stated a year ago in an airport on the way to Atlanta.

That was over twenty years ago and about a thousand face carvings back.

Carving Objective

The objective of this book is to carve a realistic Indian face and chest area in full relief from a pre-selected piece of wood. I will be carving the portion of the head that extends from the ears forward. I will also carve as large a face as the wood permits. Since the wood has been pre-selected, I will make the face fit the piece of wood.

Selection of Wood for Carving

The situation that many carvers face when finding a good piece of wood is making a carving to fit the selected piece of wood as opposed to selecting a pattern and then finding a piece of wood big enough for the carving.

There are several types of wood that could be selected to do the carving. They include cottonwood or black poplar bark, a small basswood limb section, and the end of a common tree limb. The selec-

tion could also include a block of wood, a piece of drift wood, a root section, a cypress knee, a pine knot, etc. To follow the carving process in this book, the wood you select should have dimensions similar to the piece of wood I am using, that of being longer than it is wide or deep.

The carving I am going to carve can be done in any of the above mentioned pieces of wood and while I am selecting cottonwood bark, you can select whatever kind of wood you wish to do your face in. In this book we are concerned much more with the carving techniques than with the choice of wood.

Determining the Size of the Face to be Carved

The first thing that to be done is to decide what size face can be carved in the piece of wood. The carved face is to be as large as the wood will allow and still be carved in full relief.

The most common errors that carvers make when carving faces in a long piece of wood are: 1. The faces are too long and too narrow; 2. The faces are too flat; 3. The faces are too small for the piece of wood.

Proportions of the Head and Face

A head is 5 eyes wide

The facial area, the area below the natural hairline, is divided into three equal portions: the chin to the bottom of nose; the bottom of nose to the brow line; the brow line to the natural hair line. The natural hair line is about 1\10 the length of the head.

The center of the eyes is half way between the top of the head and the chin.

There is one eye width distance between the eyes.

The corners of the mouth extend to an imaginary line drawn down from the centers of the eyes.

The bottom of the nose is about one eye width.

The portion of the head between the chin and nose is divided into three equal sections: The bottom of the chin to the top of the chin; the top of the chin to the lip line; the lip line to the bottom of the nose.

The bottom of the ears is located across from the area between the mouth and nose. The top of the ears are across from the brow line.

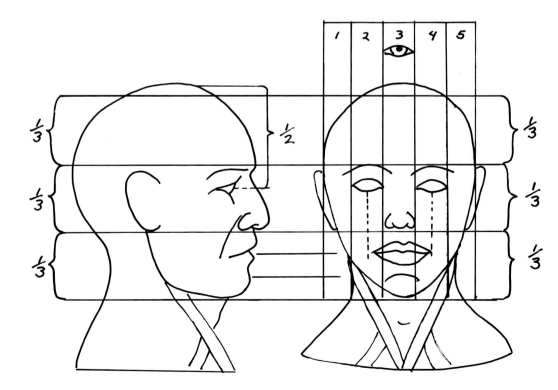

After selecting the area where you want to locate the face in the wood, draw an outline of this area on the piece of wood.

Using standard relationships that apply to heads in general, the average head will fit into a square when looking at it from the front. The average head is also about 3/4 as wide as it is high. With the hair added, the face will be as wide as it is high.

The limits of the size of the face that will be carved will be determined by the width and depth of the wood. When size is determined this way, there will be enough wood to carve the face in full relief to avoid flatness and the face will not be too long and narrow.

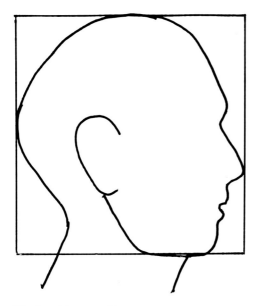

The head fits roughly into a square.

The head is about three-fourths as wide as it is deep.

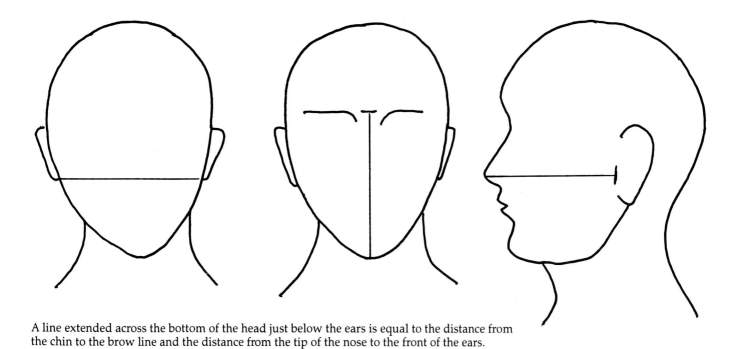

A line extended across the bottom of the head just below the ears is equal to the distance from the chin to the brow line and the distance from the tip of the nose to the front of the ears.

TOOLS & LIGHT

For any carving project, the type and condition of the carver's tools and the type of light in which the carver works is important, particularly when one is carving a realistic face. Light is one of your most valuable tools. It is impossible to carve good faces, let alone good realistic faces, when a carver works with poor carving light. It is important that you read this section on tools and light, paying special attention to the section on light, before you begin your carving.

Tools

A large collection of fancy tools is not needed for carving faces. I have been carving faces for twenty years, and as you will see from the pictures in this book, my personal tools are not very fancy nor expensive. What I have discovered, over years of trial and error, is that particular cuts are best made with certain tools. When carving, I select the tool that has proven best for a specific cut and use that tool. When carving a face, I use an average of about twenty different tools per face. If you plan to carve a lot of faces, I suggest you try to match the tools I use in this book.

Because some of the tools I use are "homemade", you might not have the same tool in your tool box. When it is not possible to match my tool, use another tool that will produce a similar cut. In general, what you need are gouges of different sweeps or curves, ranging from very deep U-shaped gouges to gouges with a very gentle curves. There should be a variety of different size tools, including some micro tools, because some of the carving cuts call for very small tools. Power tools that produce the same cuts as the gouges may be used. Personally, I rarely use power tools when carving on the actual face; I find I carve finer detail with hand tools. That is my personal preference. In carving, the only thing that counts is making the right cut. When you use the right tool for the cut, the carving process will flow faster and smoother and the end result will be a better carving.

Use the largest tool that will produce a particular cut. This concept will save you time and give you smoother cuts. A smaller tool can work adequately, but you will have to make multiple cuts to achieve the same results.

Notice that I use a large shallow gouge for all of my roughout work (*see page 12*). My roughout tool is a gouge that was originally designed to be used with a mallet. I have wrapped the blade of this gouge with strips of rubber cut from an old car inner tube (*see page 17*). The wrapped blade then becomes the handle and allows me to be able to comfortably grip the tool closer to the cutting edge. I carve with this gouge by rotating my wrist down and to the side. This allows the gouge to cut with a strong and accurate slicing motion. I often hold my other tools with "pencil grip" and wrap them with the rubber inner tubing for a better grip. Try holding your tools in these styles. These methods generate a lot of leverage, produce excellent control and are less tiring than many other ways of holding tools.

Notice in the pictures of me carving, some part of the tool hand is usually in contact with the wood. Try to have part of your carving hand in contact with the wood. This will give you more control over your cuts. You should be able to stop a cut at any time, in any portion of a cut. Learn to apply only enough pressure to your tool to execute the cut.

Carving Light

The proper use of light is rarely mentioned in carving instruction, yet it is one of the most important and useful tools that an carver uses. One must have good light when carving realistic faces because of the fine detail and subtleties inherent in the realistic face. It is impossible to carve realistic faces under poor light conditions. Carving in poor light is like trying to play a musical instrument that is out of tune, or like carving with tools that are incredibly dull. A carver with poor carving light will be unable to get good and consistent results and never be able to progress to full carving capability regardless of the subject matter.

Poor light is defused, bright and even. It is a light that does not cast shadows. Examples of poor light are the outside light of a bright overcast day or the inside light found in a shop that is brightly lit with the florescent ceiling lights. Good lighting for a wood shop is usually poor lighting for woodcarving or sculpting activities. Light that strikes a carving from the wrong direction, or light that is too dim or too bright to allow the carver to see well is inadequate for good carving. Bright light that is coming from a side direction makes a carving area look bigger and dim light makes a carving area look smaller. Carving in a light that is too bright or too dim causes a carving to be carved out of proportion.

Good light is directional and casts shadows. Good light allows the carver to see the contours of the surface of the carving by producing the proper shadowing effect. Good light creates shadows that assist the carver in seeing the detail necessary to complete the carving. Good light causes minimal visual distortion.

A simple way to achieve good lighting is to use an inexpensive swing arm lamp, as you will see. Use a bulb that is comfortable for your eyes. I generally use a 60 watt bulb. By using the swing arm of the lamp you will be able to move the lamp to a position directly in front of you and your work area. Next, position your carving (or the light) so that the light from the lamp strikes the carving at about a 45 degree downward angle and you are ready to go to work. There can be background light, but the background light must be dimmer than the light that produces the shadows you need to see on the carving.

The carving in this book was carved using the lighting just described. As much as possible, the pictures of the carving in this book were taken from the view point of the carver, enabling you to see the carving from the carvers point of view. To get the best use of this book, match your lighting with mine. Match the position of your carving and your light with the examples in the book and the shadows that are produced by the carving cuts in the book will be the same as the shadows seen on your carving.

In the carving seminars, I give the students their own swing arm lamps and keep the classroom lights dim. The students must depend on their individual lamp in order to see their work. After two days of using light like this, I ask the students to turn off their lamps. I turn up the lights in the classroom and continue the class activities. It is at this time the students dramatically realize the difference between good and bad lighting conditions. Almost immediately the class requests that the room lights be dimmed and the swing arm lamps be turned back on.

One other way to use light as a tool is by adding a dimmer control to the lamp. In carving, some cuts are best made with a normal light but some more subtle cuts are best made with a dimmer light. The dimmer control gives a carver flexibility to quickly adjust the light.

In my carving shop I have on the ceiling three banks of parallel bright florescent lights running the length of the shop. Each bank is on a different switch so I am able to dim any portion of the shop. When carving in my shop, I use my swing arm lamp with a dimmer and I usually turn off the banks of lights in front of me and those over head, keeping the bank located behind me illuminated for background lighting. When doing very fine detailed carving, I completely darken my shop and turn off all of the overhead lights and use only the swing arm lamp with a dimmer.

I encourage you to experiment with lighting. Once the best lighting for a particular carving is determined, be sure to maintain that particular light for consistent results.

Soft and Hard Cuts

A soft cut is a cut made with a tool that does not cut a thin line. A soft cut happens when two surfaces come together without showing a distinct line or separation where the two surfaces meet. Such a line is made using a V-gouge or veiner that leaves a slightly rounded area at the bottom of the cut. A soft cut does not leave a distinct line or shadow. A soft cut is used to show where surfaces meet and blend together. Most lines of the face and most planes that intersect are soft cut lines.

A hard cut is where two surfaces come together and there is a definite separation line between the two surfaces. This cut is made by using a straight blade knife to cut a V-shaped channel. There will be a sharp line where the two surfaces meet. A hard cut always leaves a distinct line or shadow. A hard cut is to show separation.

CARVING THE FACE

Select the wood. Here are some pieces of wood that could be used, they include cotton wood bark, a log of basswood, and an end of a thin log. You could also use a block of wood. On the longer pieces I tend to carve the face from the middle, showing the facial view. The shorter piece could be carved in the round.

Delineate the area that the face will be in.

I'm going to use cottonwood bark. The first thing I need to do is figure out what size face I can get out of the wood. Draw an outline of the wood at the point that you wish to carve.

Turn the piece on it side and trace the depth of the wood on a separate piece of paper.

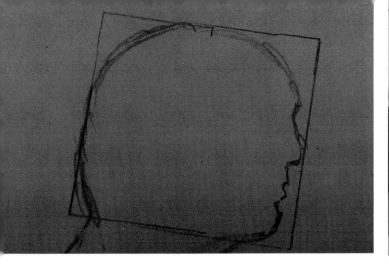

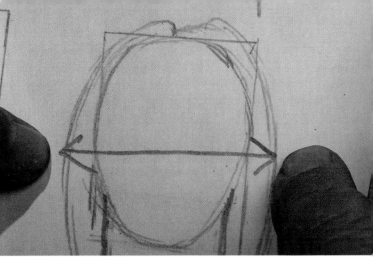

I want to make the largest face I can to fit in this depth and this width. I know a head without the hair will fit in a square area, when looked at in profile (*see page 5*).

The measurement that will govern the size of the head I can carve here is the width. One of the most common mistakes when carving in a long piece of wood like this is that carvers make the faces too long. The width dictates the length.

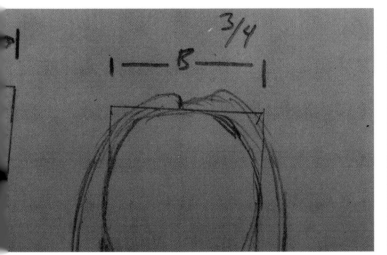

I also know that the head is approximately 3/4 as wide as it is deep. With hair added, however, it is just about as wide as it is deep.

On the outline of the wood, I draw a face based on the width of the wood, using the basic proportions of the face (*page 4*).

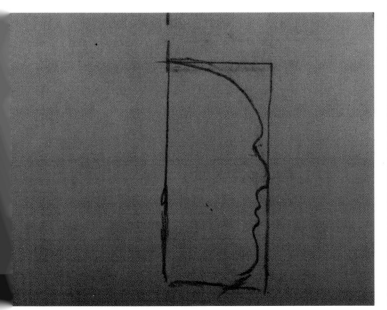

The face I will put in this wood will be in full relief, going half way back on the head, or about to the front of the ear.

The depth of face is equal to the width of the face at the bottom at the ear (*see drawing page 5*).

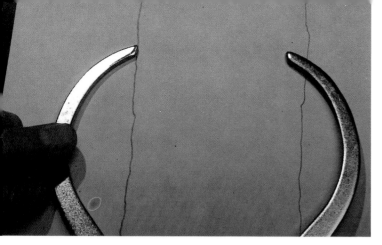

I have to have at least that much depth in the wood to put half a face on in full relief. Turning to the outline of the depth of the wood, I see there is extra so the wood is deep enough.

You can use a photograph in the same way, by drawing the grid on a copy of it, using the features as your guidelines. Add the widths of the mouth and the eyes and you have all the information you need to draw a profile and carve a figure.

Fold the front view drawing in half and transfer the measurement to the profile, before drawing the profile view (*page 11*).

The front view has been drawn using the basic proportions of the face (page 4). There are three equal areas from the hair line to the chin. The distance from the chin to the nose is divided in thirds. The width of the head at the eyes (one half way up the head) is divided in fifths to get the width and position of the eyes. The nose is the width of one eye. The ends of the mouth align with the centers of the eyes. The line of the mouth is 2/3 of the distance between the chin and the nose. These will be the guidelines.

Tape the copy to a plain sheet of paper and extend the grid. Measure from ear to ear (the head is slightly turned so we adjust shorter)...

and lay it on the grid. This is how deep the wood will need to be for carving. The width is taken from the photo.

Do the same from the nose down. This is only the best *estimate*, but it is a lot better than just whacking away at the wood with no guide. Even if you create your own face, a photograph is a good reference to have handy. It just helps you see better.

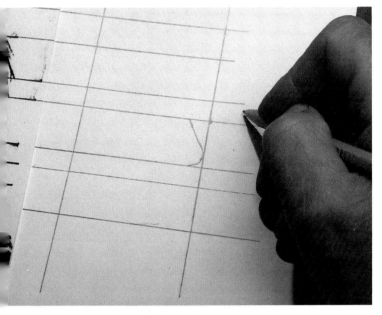

Build the profile, beginning with the nose, the point of the face that is farthest forward.

Cut a template of the profile from a piece of stiff cardboard.

Continue up from there estimating the shape of the features based on what you see in the photo.

Prepare the area for the carving. On cottonwood bark I clear off the loose exterior. On basswood I would simply remove the outer bark.

Ready for layout.

Establish the mass of the face by carving the forehead and neck.

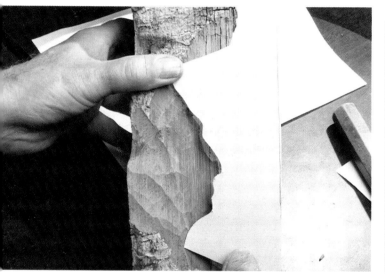

Check to make sure you still have room for the head, both width and depth.

Block in the nose and brow.

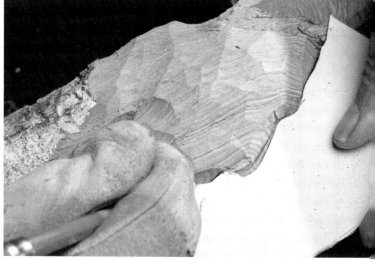

Hold the template out from the wood and roughly mark the profile.

Continue to check with the template and mark the area to carved. Remember you are establishing the general shape, not going after a final fit. The template will not fit tightly against the profile.

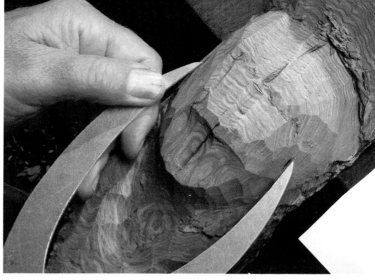

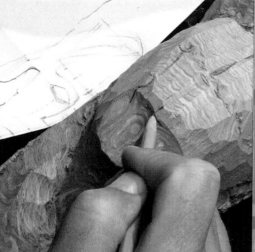

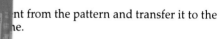

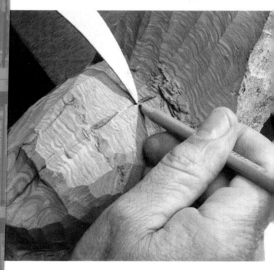

Ready to add some detail.

...nt from the pattern and transfer it to the ...e.

Draw the center line...

the head from the chin to the hairline.

Fold the pattern in half and mark the eye le... part of the face.

...irline back from the tip of the nose.

Draw in the hairline, all around the face.

Establish the slope of the forehead.

Trim the face back to the hairline. At the cheeks narrow the face to the correct width.

We are getting pretty close to having the basic shapes set.

Remove some of the excess mass beside the nose.

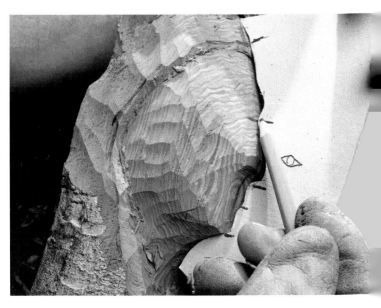

Mark the brow ridge.

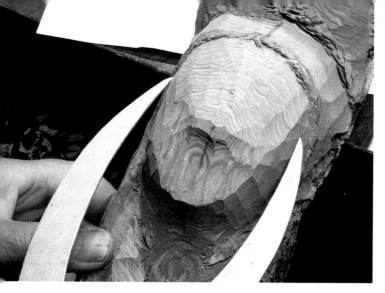

Check the width with the pattern.

Trim the carving to the correct widths.

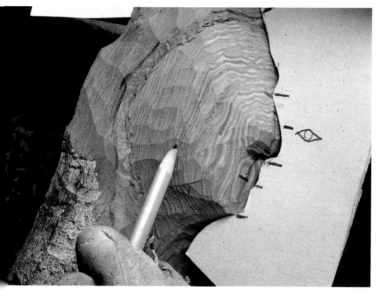

Mark the bottom of the nose and the mouth.

Scoop out the underside of the nose.

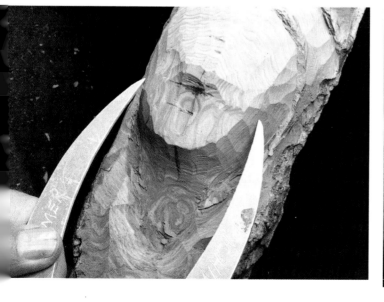

Transfer the width of the face at these points from the pattern.

The area under the nose should be a rounded cut, not sharp.

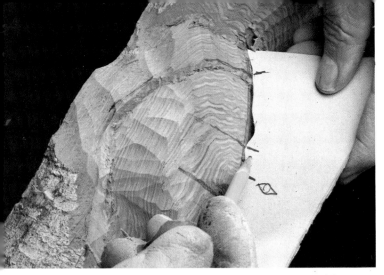

Redraw the basic reference lines. It is best to use the template to establish the position of the lines, because it conforms to the contour of the face.

Mark in the nose line and the half circles of the eye area.

Mark the eye area, which extends halfway between the nose and brow lines.

Ready to carve the major planes of the face.

Mark the width of the nose, giving it an extra 1/8" or so.

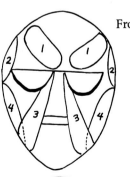
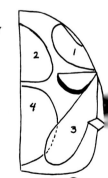

Front view   Side view

Planes and features
3/4 view

Major planes of the face.

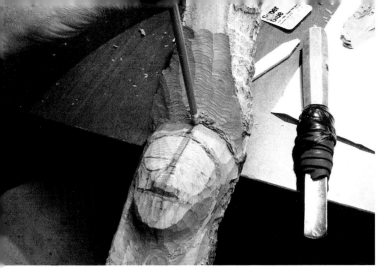

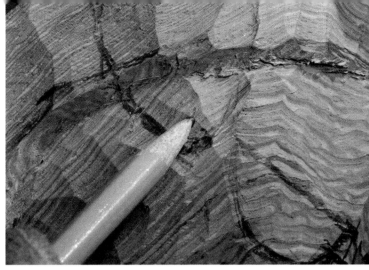

Before continuing, check your light (*see page* 7). A pencil held like the one in the photograph should cast a shadow down the center of the carving. I do this often to make sure I have things correctly aligned and symmetrical.

The temple plane starts just below the corner of the eye, right above the cheek bone, and extends back to the ear at the side of the head.

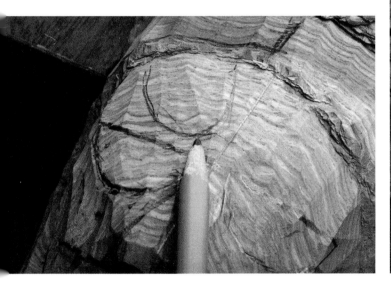

The face is divided into a number of planes. The forehead plane sweeps from the center of the forehead up and out from the brow.

Carve the temple plane with the gouge, extending it back to the hairline.

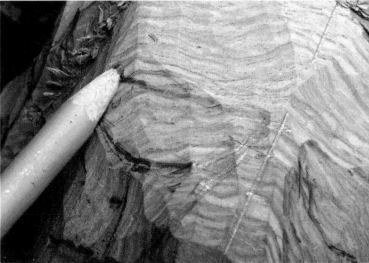

Carve the forehead planes with a broad gouge.

The juncture of the facial planes form important areas on the face, like this ridge at the brow and edge of the forehead.

17

Cut the lower eye area with a v-tool. The v-tool will help you avoid hard, sharp lines on the face. With only a couple exceptions which you'll see later, we want the lines of the face to be soft.

By cutting with only a corner of the large chisel, it functions, in effect, as a small tool.

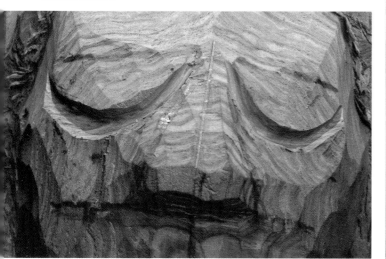

Progress.

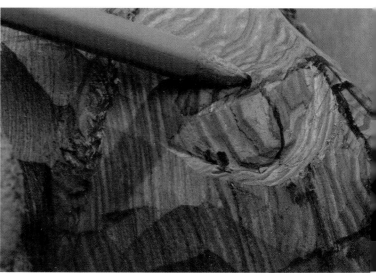

Round from the brow down and in. The eyes should have this kind of round slope if they are to look natural. Carve deeper at each end so the ends are further back than the middle.

Round off the eye areas.

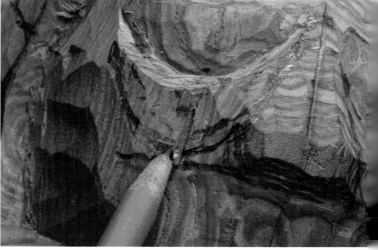

The next plane runs along the side of the nose and down to the jawline.

The cut is made with the tool running along the slant of the nose.

Carve it with a gouge.

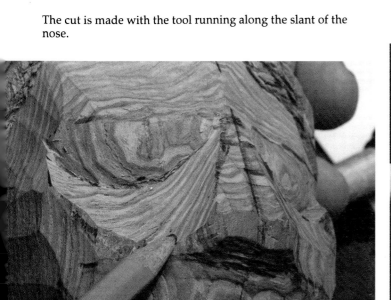

A common mistake is to make the side of the nose too angular where it meets the cheek. The side of the nose is actual a gently curved surface blending in with the cheek.

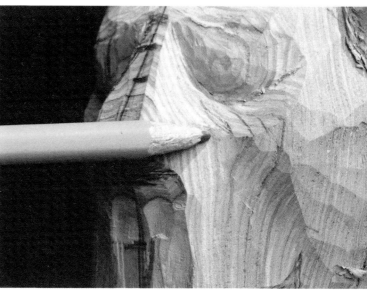

Pay attention to the juncture of the two planes. Make sure they are symmetrical on each side of the face.

This plane starts beside the nose, comes over the cheek, and back beside the jaw. It goes back as far as the back corner of the eye.

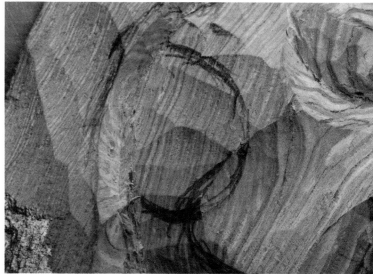

This lower plane at the back side of the cheek laps the previous plane just a little.

Carve this plane.

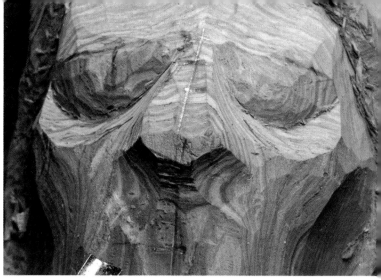

The middle of the nose is left full, with the side cuts sweeping down and out in a curve.

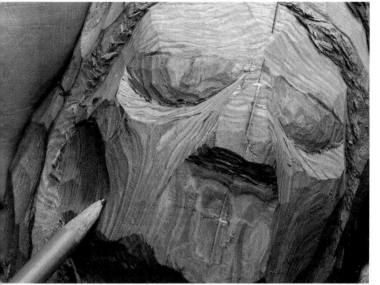

A complex shape develops when the four planes come together.

Redraw the reference lines for the chin and the mouth.

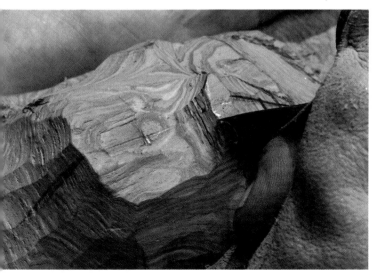

Trim away the corners of the nose to get a better perspective on your carving. This is a curved cut.

Draw in the mouth line. It is as wide as the centers of the eyes.

Draw in the arc of the chin...

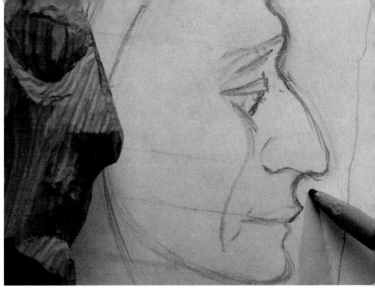

Create the curve of the underside of the nose and the upper lip.

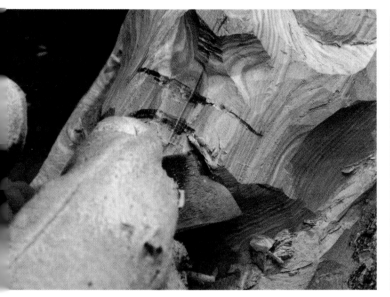

Cut up to the chin line from below...

Use a deep gouge to cut the curve. Don't take the cut too deep. If you are going to err, it is better to do it on the shallow side.

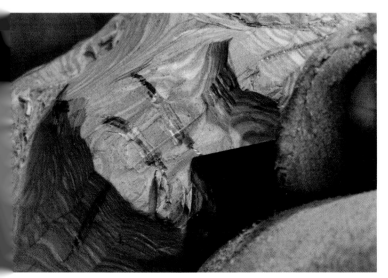

and back to it from above. I try to keep the heel of my hand in contact with the wood while carving. This stabilizes the cut. This top cut will come from the mouth line to the chin.

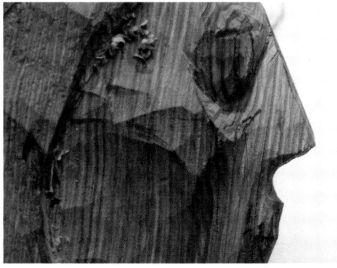

The result.

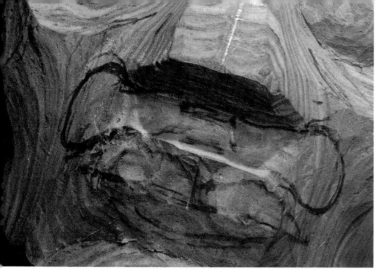

To bring out the mouth mound we need to establish planes above the upper lip. Leave the darkened area in the center alone.

This cut is angled away from the nose and toward the mouth. It picks up the dished shape of the gouge, and the bottom of the cut blends into the cheek.

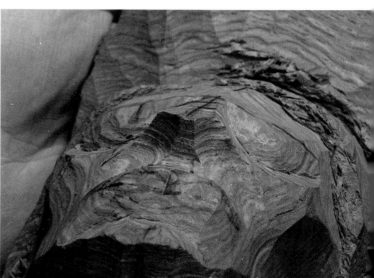

Carve the planes of the upper lip.

This forms a nice wedge in the center of the under side of the nose.

Carving the nose begins with lifting the corners. The wings of the nostrils should be higher on the face than the bottom of the nose.

At this point, look ahead and see the finished feature onpage 31. Look for the finished nose and study the steps backwards. The nose is to be narrowed next. The nose ends in a round ball-like area.

Trim around the ball of the nose.

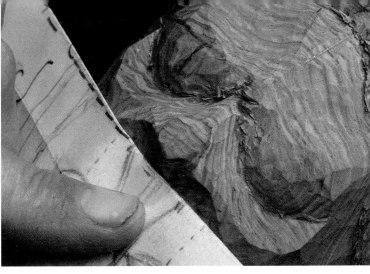

Move to the sides of the nostril. Fold your pattern and use it to mark the width of the nose.

Narrow and shape the nose up to the brow.

Come around the back of the nostril with a v-tool.

Progress.

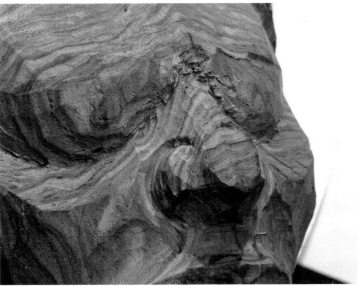

The result.

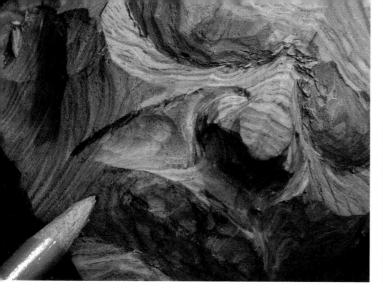

Extend the curves down the cheek until they are even with the corners of the mouth. Have you looked ahead?

The result. The cut blends in with the cheek.

Follow the line with a v-tool.

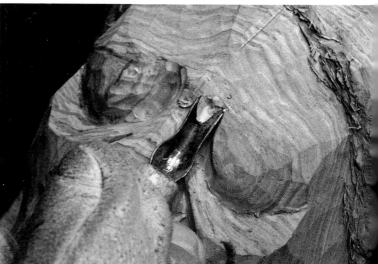

We need to lengthen the nose. This is done by raising the brow line, and involves lowering the inside of the eye. Be careful not to make the bridge of the nose too thin.

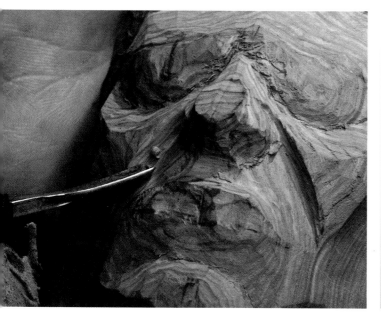

Carve the lip area back to the contour.

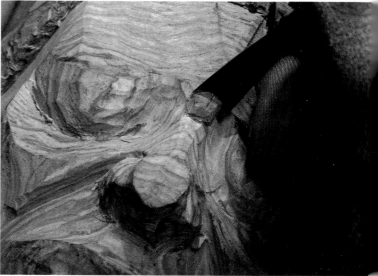

Shape the bridge of the nose.

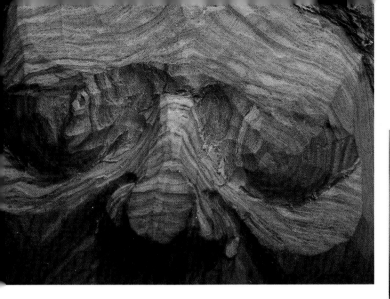

The result.

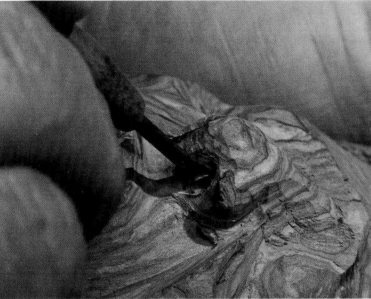

and cut them out. The hole has rounded edges, not sharp.

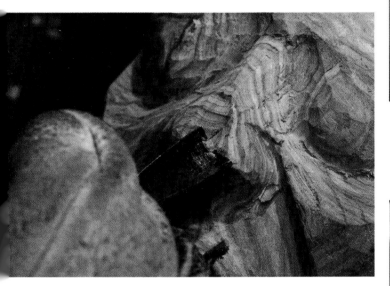

Round off the end of the nose.

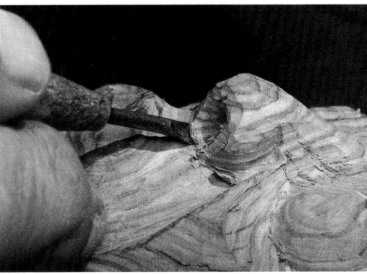

The lip runs up into the nostril. Be careful not to make the walls of the nose too thin. At this point I would suggest you get a mirror and look at the bottom of your nose...then go look at someone else's. Keep the mirror handy. It will be very useful as we do the rest of the features.

Having gone forward, you already know what the nostrils will look like, but pay attention...they are tricky! Draw them in...

Bring the line of the nostril around the back for this result. On the nose ridge there are two indentations. The top is where the cartilage meets the bone and the bottom is where the upper cartilage meets the lower cartilage.

This is the view from the bottom. Remember not to make the walls of the nostril too thin.

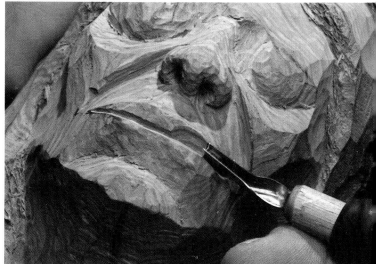

With the v of the tool in the groove, use the upper edge of the tool to shape the surface of the upper lip. Come to the middle first, giving the surface its characteristic bow shape.

Run a v-tool across the line of the mouth to set the line.

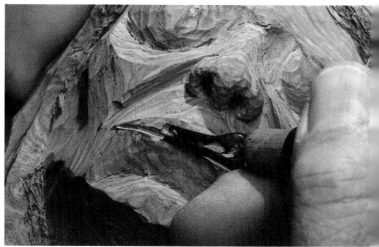

Work from the middle to the opposite corner in the same way.

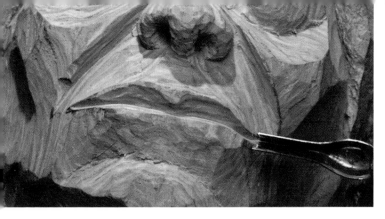

Come across the bottom lip using the lower edge of the tool, dipping to cut in its center.

and beneath the middle to bring the lip out.

Trim the corners of the mouth so they seem to come under the upper lip.

Progress.

With a gouge, deepen the contour below the lower lip.

Create a plane from the corner of the upper lip back to the flange of the nostril.

Come under the sides of the lip...

The result.

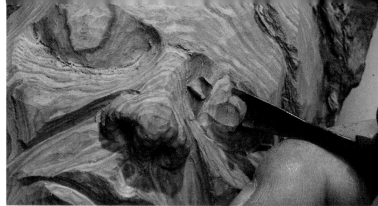

Create the philtrum.

Round the eye mounds to prepare them for the eyes.

The result. The brow needs to be a little more prominent.

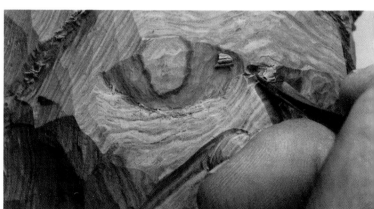

To do this we deepen the bridge of the nose.

The result. A realistic contour has been formed for the lips and the area surrounding the mouth.

Draw in the center line of the eyes.

28

This enables you to set them symmetrically. At this point it is easy to see mistakes and correct them. The figures left eye is slanting up much too much.

and lower lines of the eye oval. Notice how the upper lid continues beyond the lower at the corners.

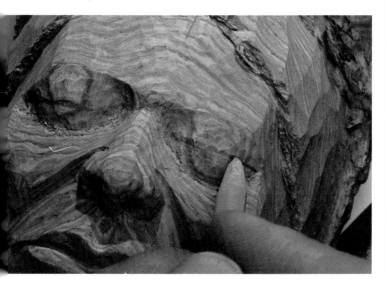

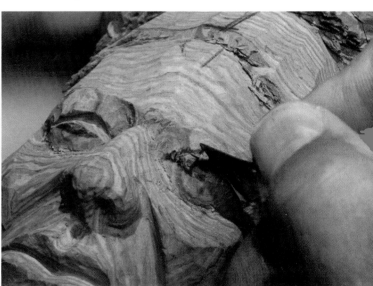

Correct the center lines until they appear natural and symmetrical.

With a gouge, cut into the line of the upper lid and back to it from the eyeball.

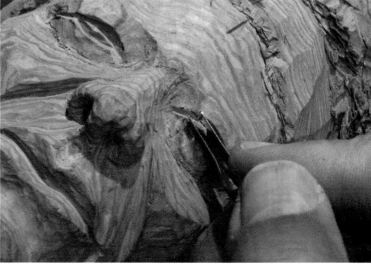

Draw the upper...

Cut on the line of the lower lid with a v-tool.

Progress.

Round the eyeball.

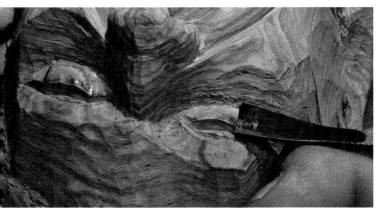

Round the lower lids...

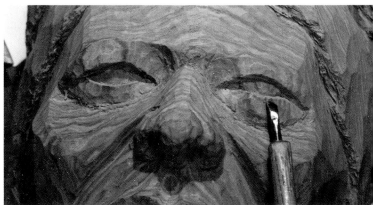

I use a micro-skew for this fine work.

and cut the outside corners back to the upper lid, so they appear to tuck under.

Define the line of the eyelid with a v-tool. This is a distinct but soft line. Too sharp a line and the eyes will look like they are popping out of their sockets.

Open the inside corners for the tear ducts.

Use a gouge to contour the upper lids...

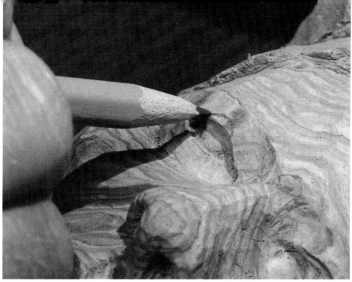

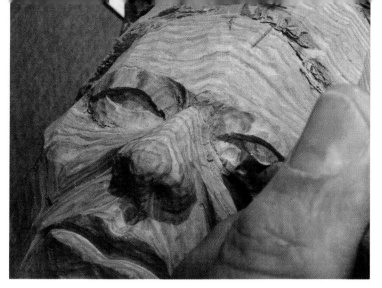

and the lower.

Continuing with the eyes, we need to establish the iris. To do this, a draw a complete circle, continuing it over the upper lid. This helps in the accuracy of size and placement.

The result.

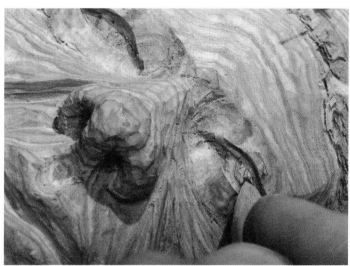

With sculpted eyes like this, which are not going to be painted, the eye must be representational. For my eyes I basically hollow out the iris, leaving a triangle of wood to represent a glint of light. I find this gives the eyes the life I want them to have. Draw two lines down from the upper lid that meeting at a point in the center of the iris. I suggest you visit museums and see what methods other sculptors have used to represent the pupil and iris.

The basic lines and contours of the face are now established. Still to carve are the details that make the face come alive.

Cut straight into these lines.

31

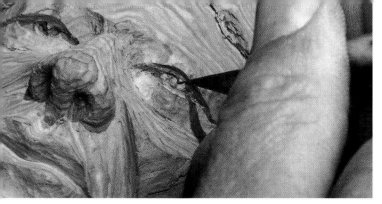

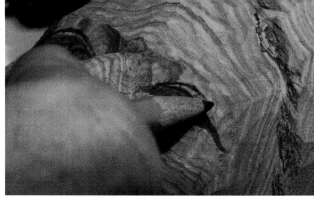

Cut wings from the upper ends of the lines along the edge of the upper lid to the line of the iris. These will act as stops.

Draw in the fold of the upper eyelid.

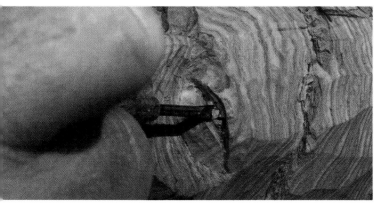

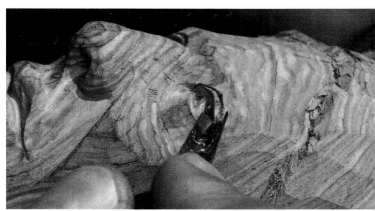

Carve out the iris around the triangle...

Carve along this line with a v-tool.

for this result.

This is the result.

One of the few hard lines on a face is the line between the lips. Cut along it with a knife, the blade following the surface of the upper lip.

Clean up the eyeball.

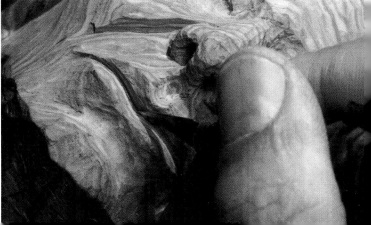

Come back to this cut from below, taking out the thin slice that defines the separation.

Prepare the surface and block the outer contours of the hair.

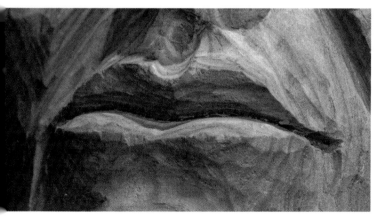

Open up the corner of the mouth...

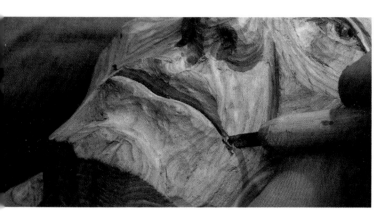

for this result.

Ready for the hair and decorative effects (*see page 44*).

I will have a center part, cut with the chisel.

Though I try to stay authentic to the traditional Indian costume, there is some creative latitude in designing the dress. Here I think I will have large round earrings.

Establish the flow of the hair down the chest. This carving will have large, wrapped braids. For now I am just setting general lines without being locked in to a final hairstyle.

Bring down the area of the chest between the hair lines.

and shape the neck back to it.

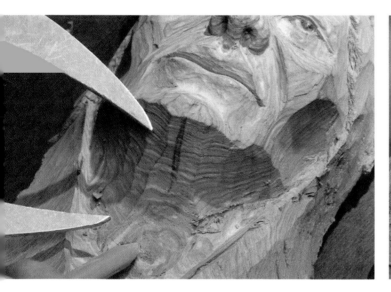

Establish the neckline of the tunic.

Use a gouge to form the large muscles that extend from behind the ear to the collar bone.

Progress. I have also made an indentation in the hairline where a decorative wrap will begin.

Cut a stop in the neckline...

Looking at the piece, I think the hair needs to come back from the face a little more at the side, so I draw the new line...

Begin to round the lower hair. Again this will be a wrapped braid, so it should be fairly round.

and carve the area away.

With a v-tool cut the lower edge of the hair wrap.

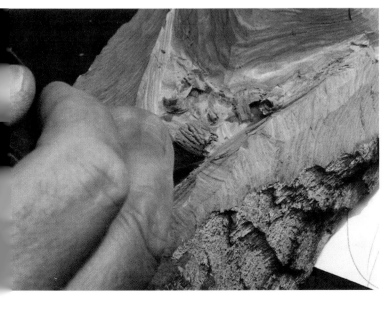

Clean up the neck area.

Clean the shoulder beside the wrap.

With large v-tool establish the line between the hair and the forehead, making it a soft line cut.

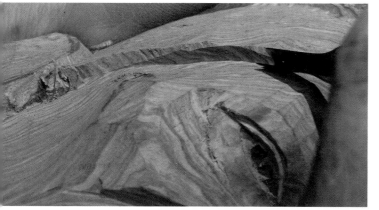

Switch to a smaller v-tool and make the angles more distinct.

Do the same at the neckline of the tunic.

Follow the lower hair line below the temples with a knife, making a clean stop cut.

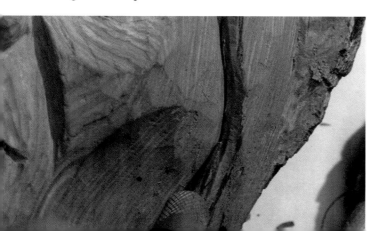

Come back to the first line with a second, cutting out a fine slice of wood that clearly distinguishes the hair line.

At the neckline use a similar method. The first cut should be made with the blade flat against the neck.

Cut back to the first cut at an angle so the cut ends up out of sight.

Now continue the curve of the neck into the cut.

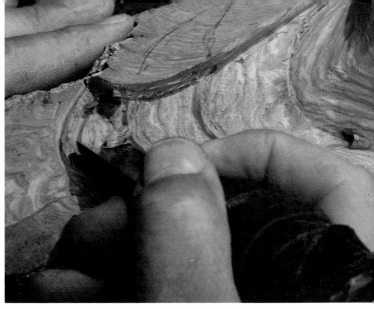

Drop the chest to the level of the bead grooves. Keep the contour of the chest.

The necklaces drape from the neck and shoulder. Each strand has it own line of draping, and must be visualized to be drawn correctly. After you draw them, move back and check them out from a distance. Make any adjustments.

Under cut the feather so it appears to rest on top of the beads.

With a v-tool cut above and below each line of beads.

Do the same under the hair wrap.

Round the edges of the beads with sandpaper. If they were larger, I would probably use a gouge to round them.

Draw in the beads. The separations of the beads need to radiate from the center of the arc of the necklace. You have to imagine that as you draw. I like to start with the center bead and work my way out.

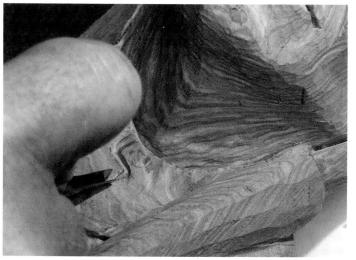

To break up the wide area of the neckline, I am going to add a button.

With a small v-tool cut across the top of the beads.

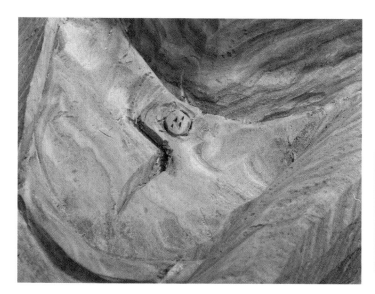

The result.

Turn the piece over, lay the tool in the groove and continue the line across the bottom of the beads.

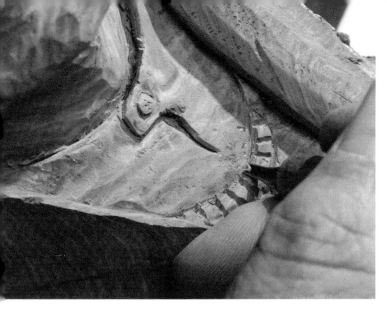

With the same tool, come straight down between the beads along the top and bottom edge.

This is a wrapped braid. It has fur around it and it is tied. There is a leather tie at the top, continuing into a leather thong that wraps in a spiral. Each spiral gets closer together as it moves toward the bottom. There is another tie at the bottom. The inward slant of the spiral keeps the eye drawn to the center of the carving.

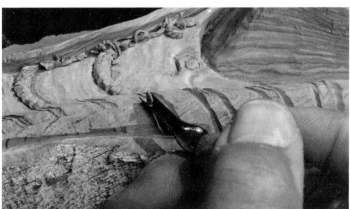

Clean up the chest around the beads, while undercutting them just a little to lift the back edge from the surface.

Carve beside the edges of the spiral, rolling around.

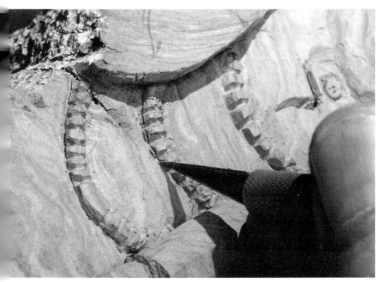

Make a light separation cut with the knife, top and bottom.

Make a separation cut along the edge of the braid.

Finish the lines of the wrap with the knife, so they appear to continue around the braid.

Go over the surface of the leather straps with a fairly flat gouge to give it a cupped appearance.

Make a straight cut down the groove.

Progress.

Create the texture of the fur. I use a power tool, though you could use a gouge. This gives a finer result. The bit is a dental burr.

Contour the edges of the fur back to the straps, giving the fur spiral a puffy look as it is puckered by the strap.

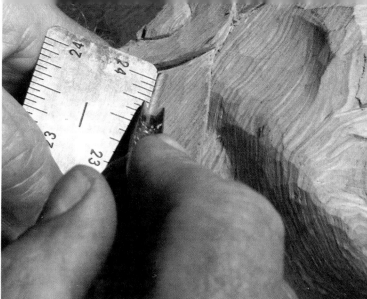

Moving to the hair ornament, draw a center circle and go around it with a v-tool. Cut back to the center circle from the larger circle, giving the surface some contour.

With a small gouge, cut along the sides of the quill. A metal ruler bends enough to be used as a guide for these cuts.

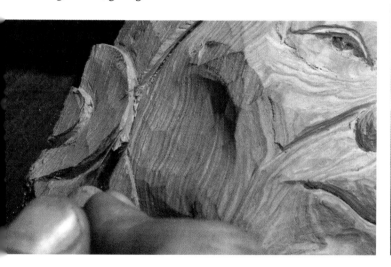

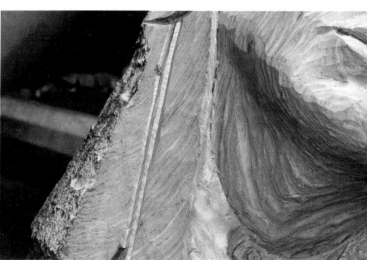

Undercut the edge of the ornament to lift it up.

Draw the quill of the feather.

Deepen the cut with a small v-tool.

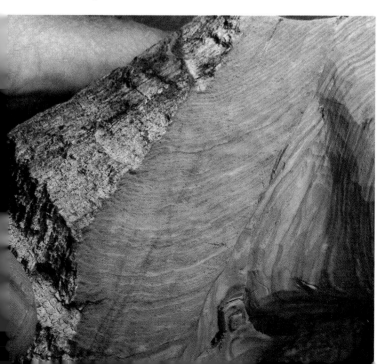

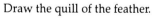

Bring the vane surface down to the level of the groove. Contour the surface with sandpaper.

Use a micro gouge to texture the vanes of the feather. Notice how my finger is beside the tool to give it direction.

A few decorations in the hair piece and the feather is done.

Continue on both sides of the quill.

Go back and refine the face. Keep the basic things you had before, but refine and smooth.

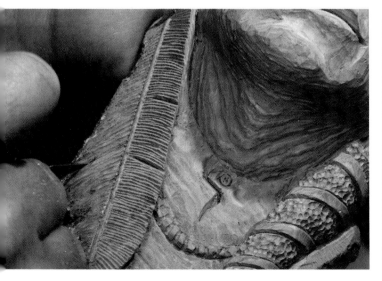

Add a couple breaks to the feather by widening the gap between selected grooves and deepening the cut with the knife.

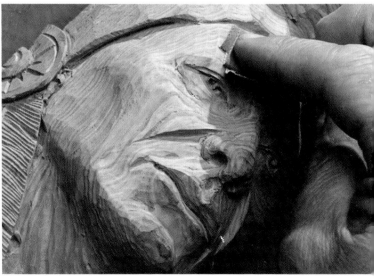

Sand lightly with 220 grit paper for softer knife cuts.

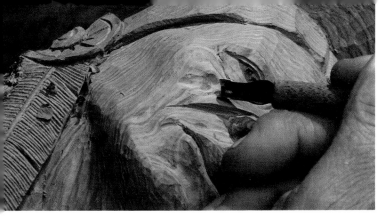

You may wish to add some detail like this smile muscle under the cheek.

Two cuts come up into the brow from the sides of the nose.

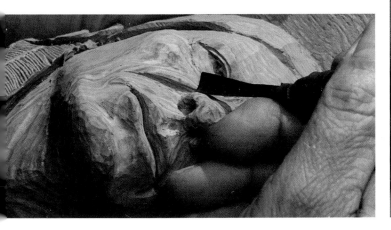

Soften any hard lines.

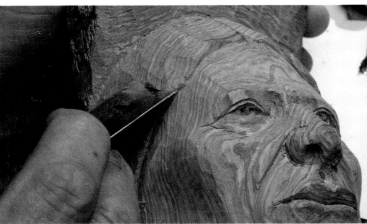

Begin the hair by getting rid of the dips and the valleys. Set the flow and shape of the overall hair mass.

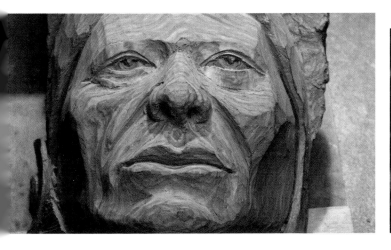

See how the left side is more refined than the right. The best way to add this detail is to find pictures and copy the features you like.

Do not try to cut each individual hair. With a gouge create the major lines of the hair. The high areas between the knife cuts represent the individual strands of hair.

Carve above the brow to bring out the forehead.

Using a v-tool, you can add some accent lines.

The carving is finished. These
views give you various perspec-
tives on the carving. When working
on a piece like this it is good to
view it from every conceivable
angle.

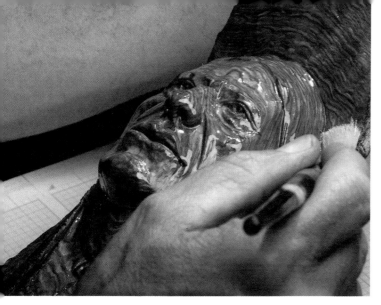

Totally seal the carving with Deft™ lacquer. It may take 4 to 8 thin coats to be certain it is totally sealed.

Brush away any dust.

Sign the piece.

When carving I depend on a single source of light to create that shadows that allow me to see details in the work. In finishing I get the same effect by using a final coat of black paint. When rubbed away, it leaves dark accent shadows in the places where I want them. The paint is an oil tube paint, thinned to form an antiquing wash. Before this step, the piece must be completely sealed with the Deft™ which has dried for 24 hours.

Starting with the face, give the carving an even, solid coat of the thinned black paint.

When the final coat is thoroughly dry, rub it down with 0000 steel wool.

Cover all carved surfaces.

Do a final rub with a lint-free cotton cloth.

After the paint has been applied, begin to rub it away with a clean cloth.

Apply a second coat of thicker black paint to the hair, which is to be a solid black.

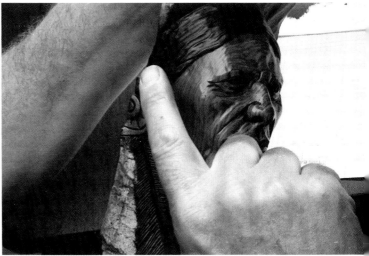

Use a clean dry brush to get into the nooks and crannies where the cloth won't reach.

Create highlights by using your finger to rub away paint from the top of the hair ridges.

Finished.

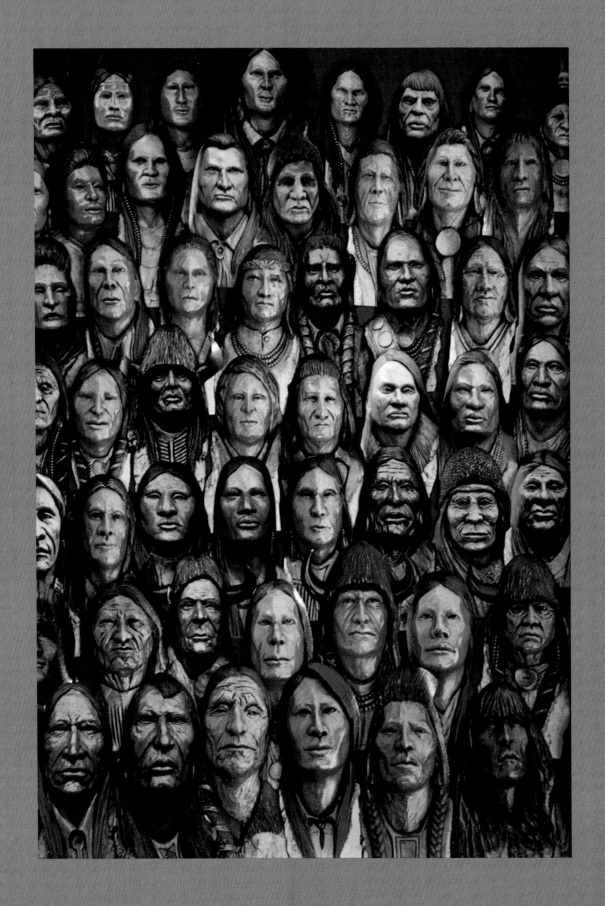

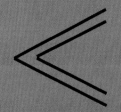
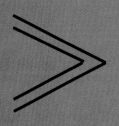

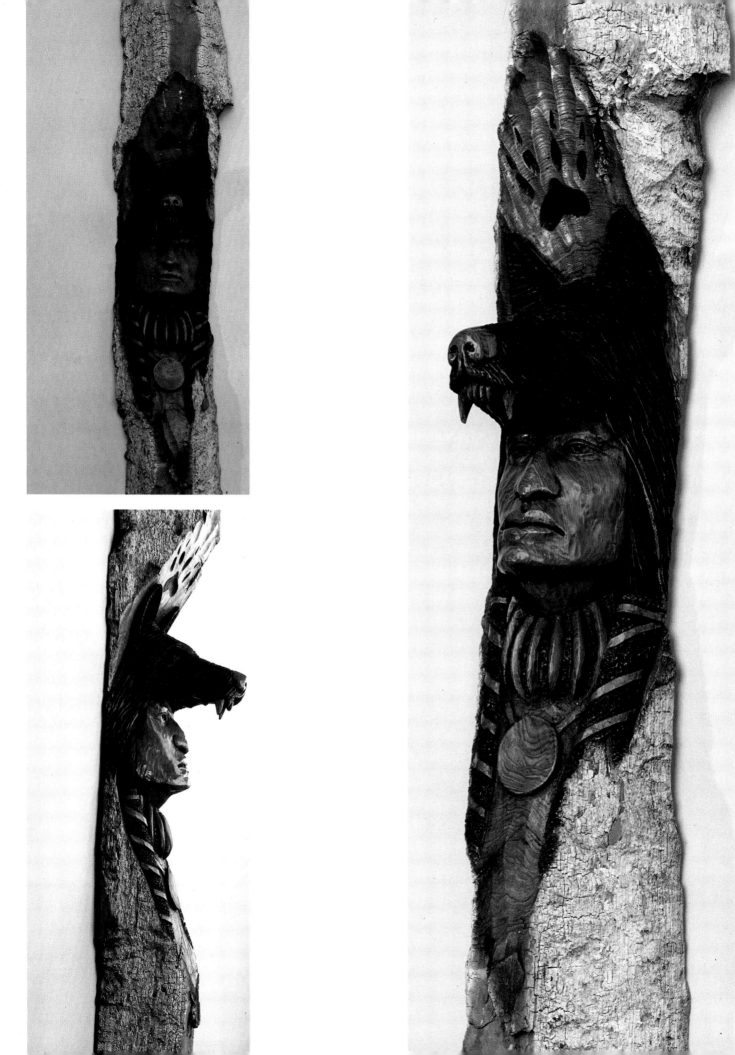